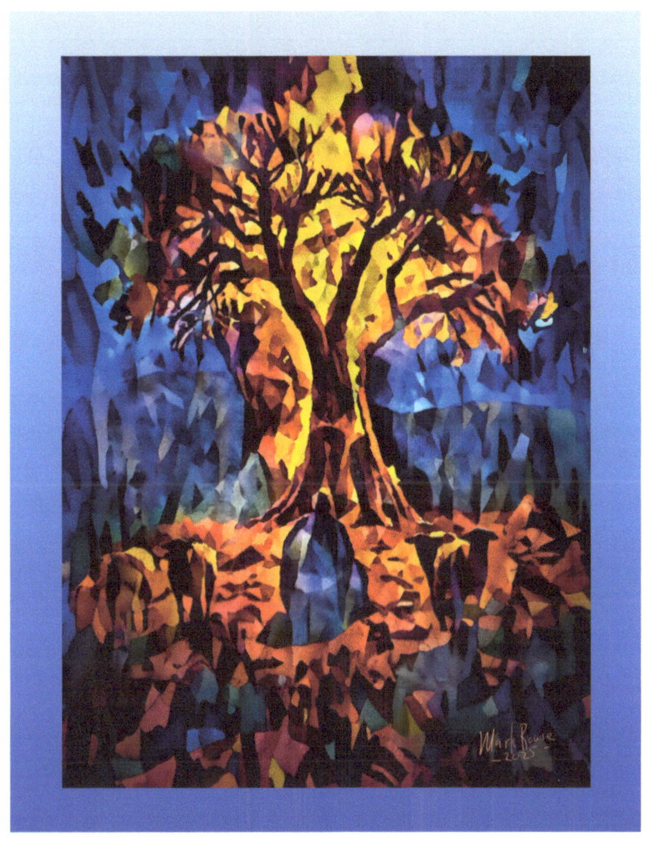

I AM...

by Mark Rouse

Why "I AM"......

Moses had no place to go —as an Israelite who had been raised in the Egyptian palace, it was not likely that he would be protected by the Israelites. The Egyptians wanted to kill him because he had killed an Egyptian for beating an Israelite. He left Egypt, his family, and his people. Facing the prospect that he could never return home, he settled in the land of Midian, where he lived as a shepherd. After forty years, at the age of 80, God came to Moses to reveal His plan. After seeing a bush that was burning but not consumed (portrayed on the cover of this book), God told Moses that He had been chosen as the instrument to free the Children of Israel. After forty years, Moses wasn't sure if he had any credibility in Egypt; he needed to be able to show and tell Pharoah and the Children of Israel why he was there.

"Who shall I say sent me?" God replied with HIS Name:

I AM who I AM.....

Spring forward to the Gospel of John. Seven time we se Jesus saying "I AM" in a way to show who He was, and reveal His nature.
In early 2025 I was asked to create a painting for a show at a large church in Indianapolis. The first painting completed in the series was "The Good Shepherd". Having never been a shepherd, I chose to research the role of shepherds in the Bible. That was quite a revelation, but as part of that research, I found the seven metaphors that Jesus used to describe Himself. This was the inspiration of the seven paintings in the "I AM Project".

I hope you find them meaningful.....

Contents

<h1>I AM.....</h1>

I AM...

...the Door

"I am the door; if anyone enters through Me, he will be saved, and will go in and out and find pasture." **John 10:9 NASB**

The Door powerfully conveys a message of welcome and spiritual invitation, centered on the figure of Jesus standing in an open doorway. Rather than blocking entry, the door serves as an open passage, inviting all to come in and experience the peace, healing, and presence of God. Jesus stands bathed in warm, ethereal light, his left hand raised gently and his right hand extended downward in a gesture of blessing and invitation, embodying openness and grace.

 The robes he wears—earthy browns, soft yellows, and luminous whites—express both humility and sanctity, reinforcing the sense of a compassionate guide who beckons those outside to enter a space of sacred promise. Behind him, rich textures and deep shades of blue, purple, and green emphasize the doorway as a vibrant threshold, not a barrier, but a symbol of transition into a place of spiritual refuge.

 This artwork invites viewers to reconsider the concept of the door—not as a restriction, but as a welcoming entrance to a renewed relationship with God.

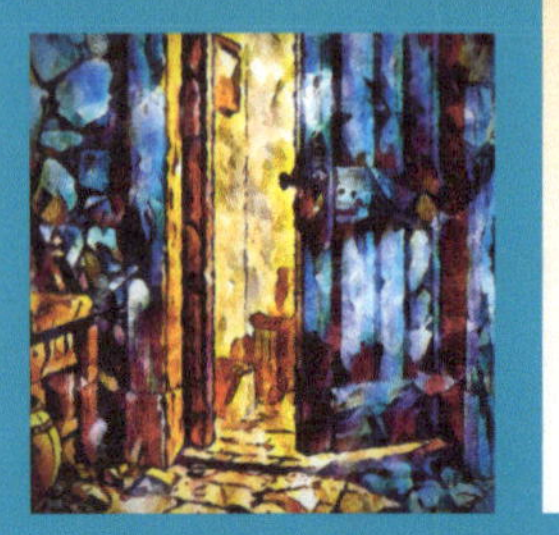

It reflects the profound meaning behind Jesus' declaration, "I AM the Door," transforming it into a beacon of hope and an open call to step beyond fear and hesitation into divine invitation and grace.

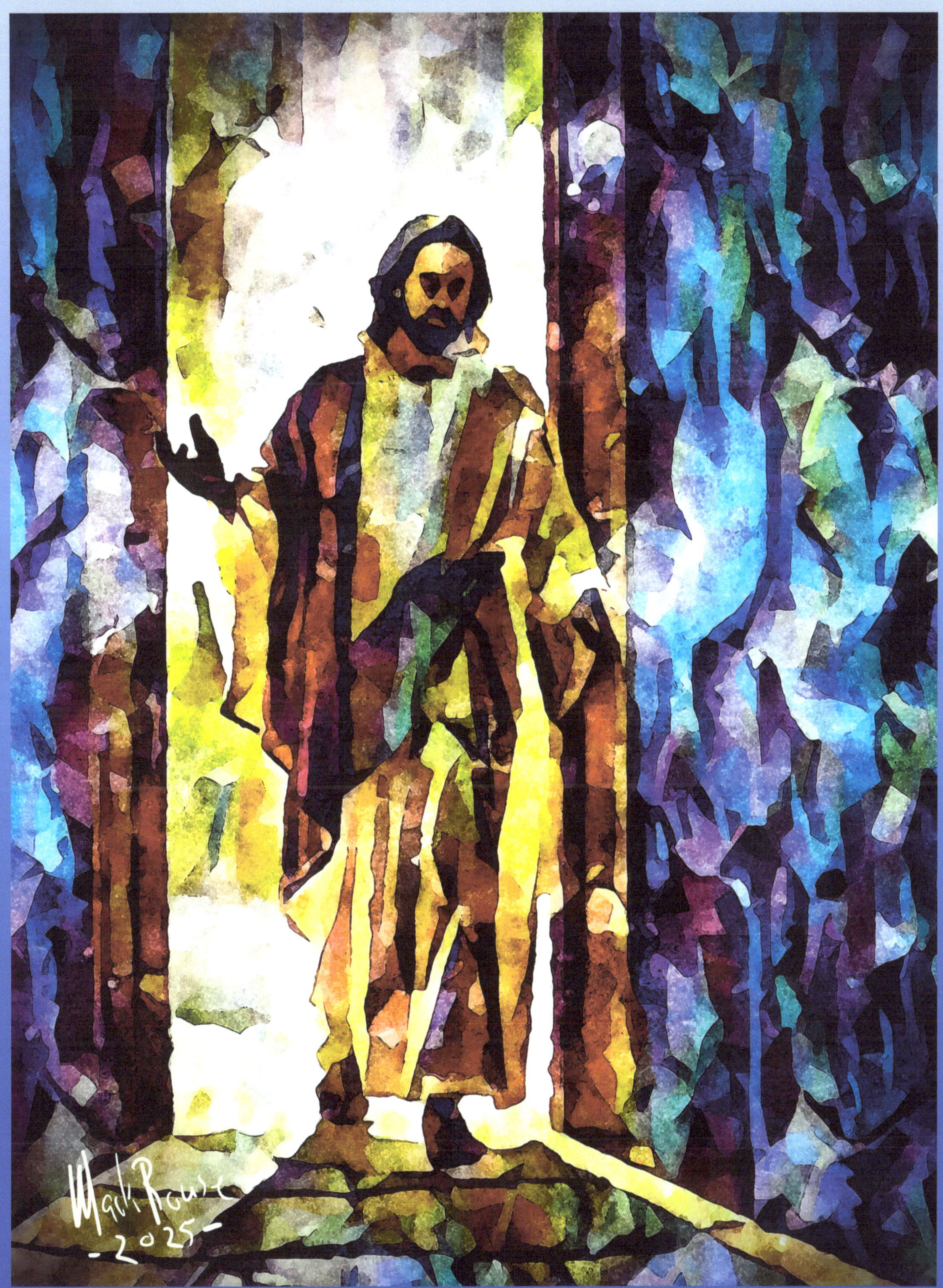
Mark Rowe
-2025-

I AM...

...the Light of the World

Then Jesus again spoke to them, saying, "I am the Light of the world; the one who follows Me will not walk in the darkness, but will have the Light of life." **John 8:12 NASB**

The Light of the World embodies a profound spiritual message drawn from the Gospel of John, where Jesus declares, "I AM the Light of the World," and echoes the promise that "Your Word is a Light Unto My Feet." This mixed media artwork visualizes the divine illumination that guides the believer's path, representing Christ as the light breaking through darkness to lead and sustain us.

At the heart of the composition, beams of radiant light symbolize God's glory shining upon Christ, who is portrayed as the source of guidance and truth. A solitary figure, wrapped in warm, glowing hues, walks along a path through a forest steeped in deep, contemplative shadows—an embodiment of the spiritual journey toward clarity and faith. The interplay of light and shadow speaks to the dynamic relationship between divine revelation and human response, inviting viewers to reflect on their own walk toward spiritual understanding.

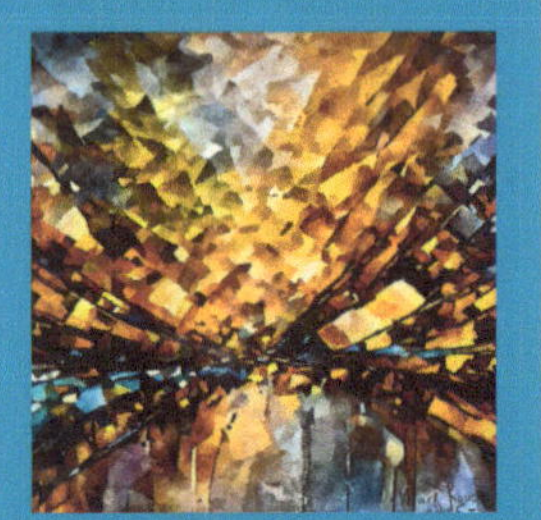

This piece powerfully unites the concepts of Light, God's Word, and the Path of Life into a single image that encourages meditation on grace, hope, and perseverance. It is a visual prayer, illustrating how divine truth illuminates the way forward even amid mystery and uncertainty.

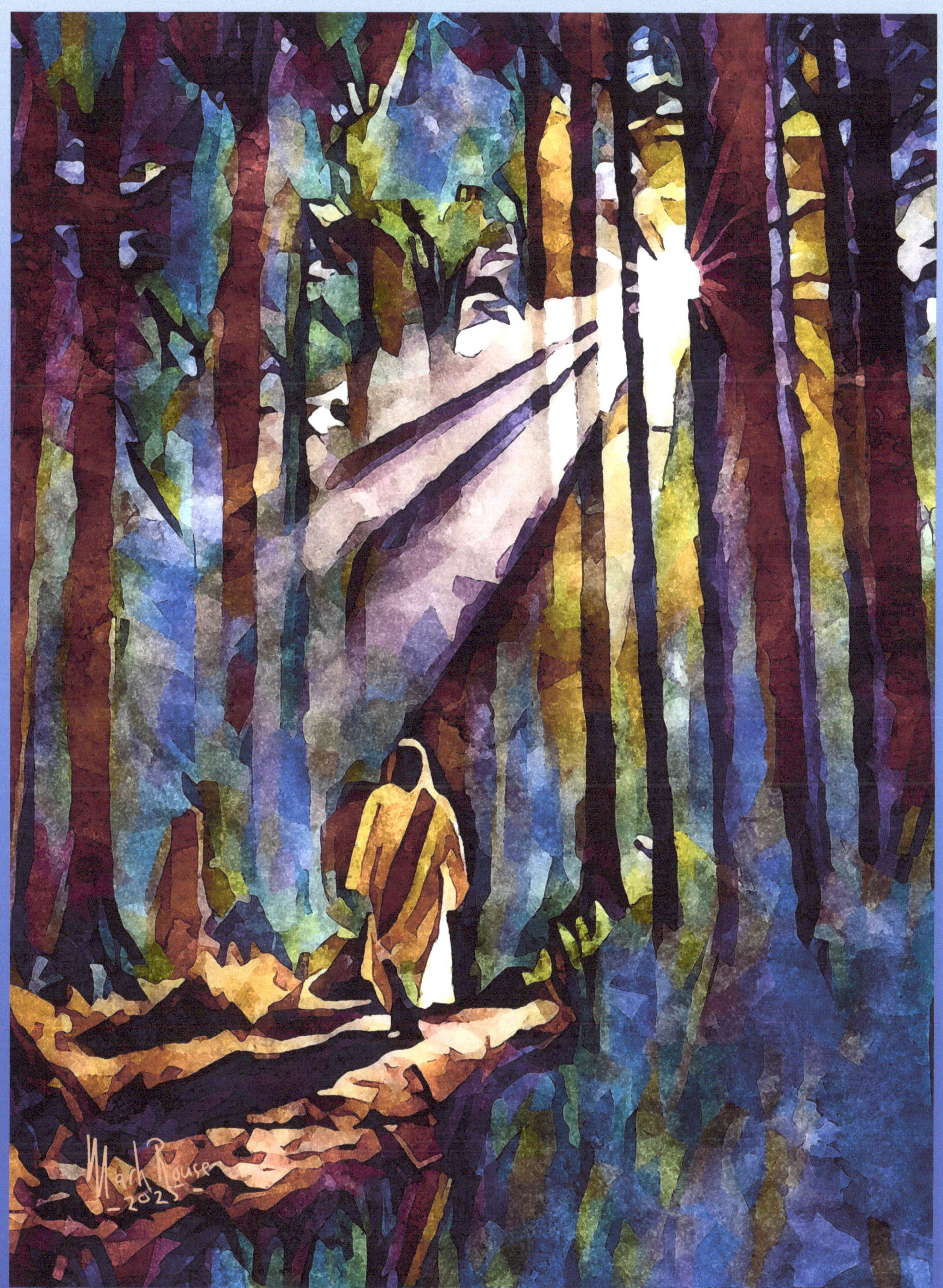

I AM...

...the True Vine

"I am the vine, you are the branches; the one who remains in Me, and I in him bears much fruit, for apart from Me you can do nothing." **John 15:5 NASB**

The True Vine invites reflection on the spiritual journey of growth, renewal, and care through the enduring symbol of the vine. At its heart stands the Vine Dresser, a contemplative figure who carefully holds a cluster of ripe grapes, embodying the role of one who nurtures and prunes with patience and purpose. His attentive presence reminds us that pruning is not punishment but a vital act of renewal—encouraging future fruitfulness and sustaining life.

 The vine, stretching vertically with abundant leaves and heavy clusters of grapes, represents the source of strength and support for all branches, fruitful or not. This relationship reflects the deeper truth that growth depends on connection and care beyond immediate productivity.

 Surrounding the Vine Dresser is a luminous background of blended blues, purples, yellows, and greens, creating an atmosphere that is both earthly and transcendent. Realistic details anchor the scene, while impressionistic

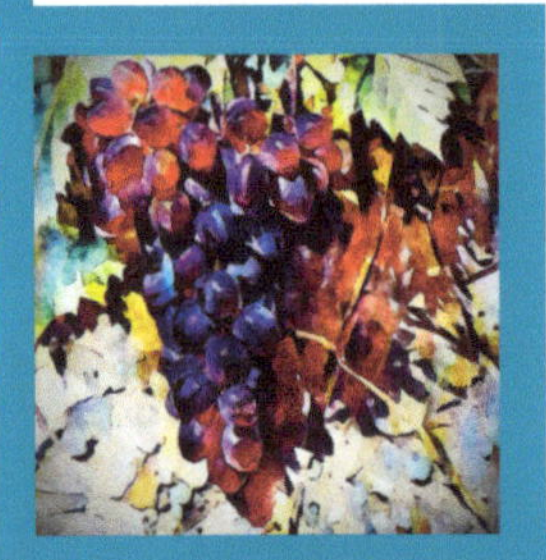

light and color express the unseen grace and spirit at work in the cycle of care and transformation. The True Vine calls viewers to contemplate the patience, love, and renewal inherent in the spiritual process of tending life's vineyard.

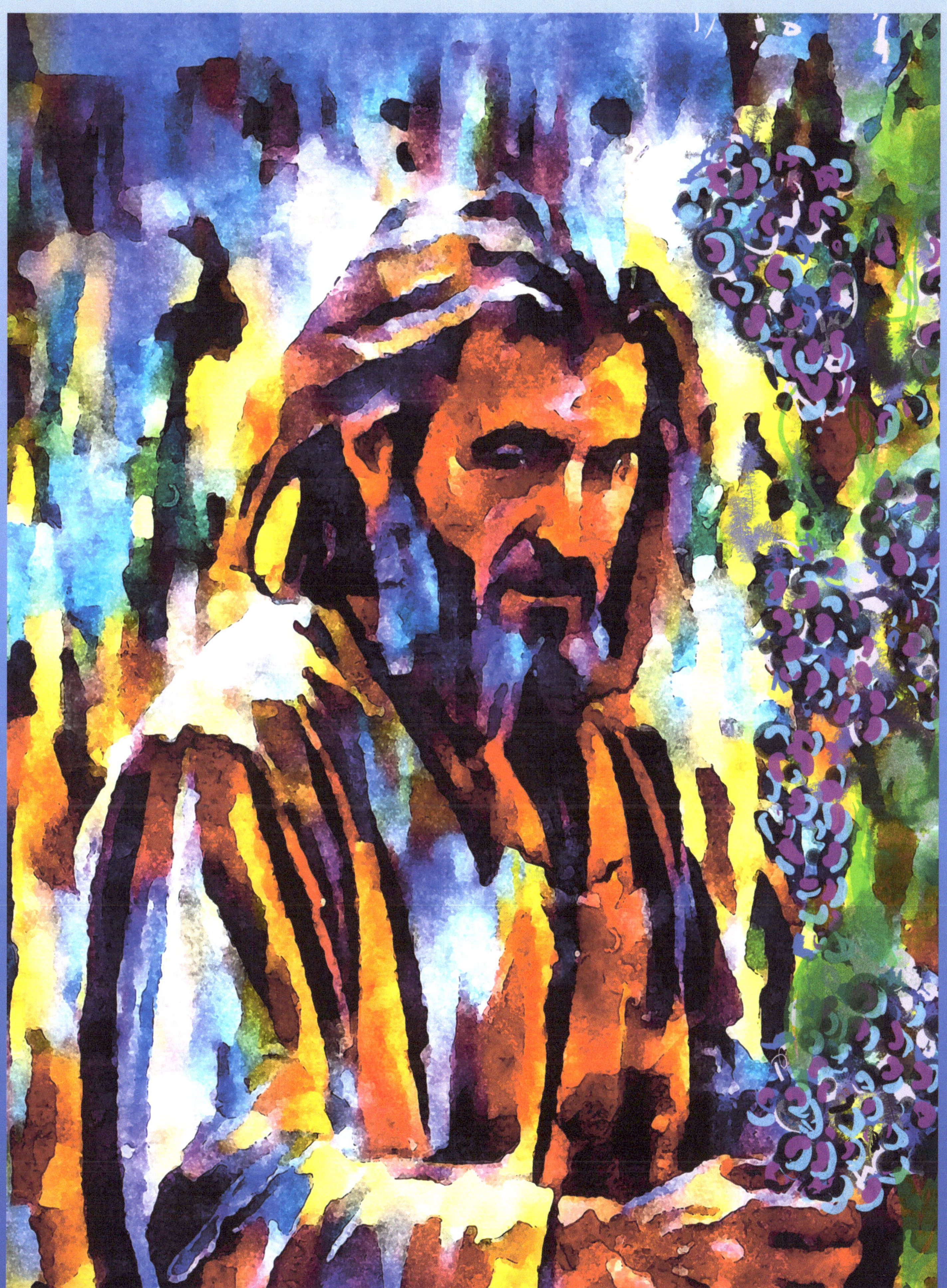

I AM...

...the Good Shepherd

"I am the good shepherd, and I know My own, and My own know Me, just as the Father knows Me and I know the Father; and I lay down My life for the sheep. And I have other sheep that are not of this fold; I must bring them also, and they will listen to My voice; and they will become one flock, with one shepherd." **John 10:14-16 NASB**

The Good Shepherd presents a vivid and contemplative moment woven into a rich, layered landscape where tradition and symbolism converge. At the forefront stands a solitary shepherd clad in a flowing red robe and blue cloak, his presence calm yet resolute as he holds a staff—a timeless emblem of guidance and care. Surrounding him, a flock of sheep moves quietly, embodying trust and dependency within the expansive and colorful environment. The scene unfolds in a dynamic interplay of blues, purples, greens, and reds, where bold brushwork and fluid color transitions evoke a sense of depth and subtle motion that invites the viewer to linger.

In the background, a gently ascending path leads the eye toward three hilltop crosses, anchoring the composition within a spiritual framework. This thoughtful inclusion connects the shepherd's watchful gaze not to himself but to a greater sacrifice beyond the frame, revealing a layered narrative about faith, responsibility, and the quiet strength found in understanding one's role within a larger story. The decision to omit the figure of Jesus and instead focus on another shepherd enriches the piece with introspection, suggesting shared reverence and recognition of the cost of protection.

Executed in mixed media, the artwork balances texture and fluidity, merging painted and layered elements that enhance its stained-glass quality and deepen its visual 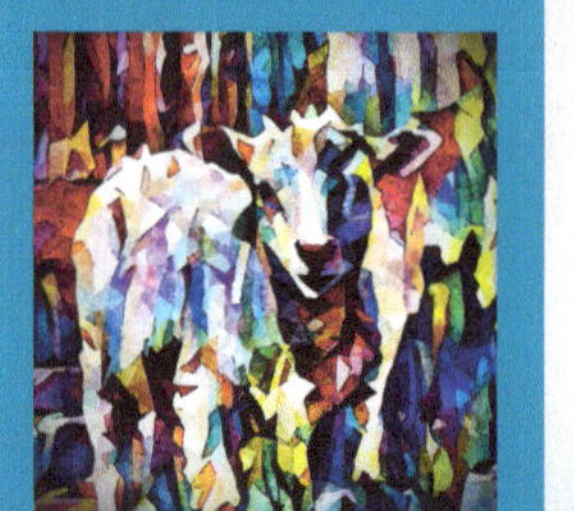 resonance. This work stands as a reflection on guidance and sacrifice, encouraging contemplation of both visible and unseen connections within the cycle of faith and care. It invites viewers to recognize the steadfast presence of those who lead with humility amidst challenges, grounded in enduring spiritual themes that transcend time.

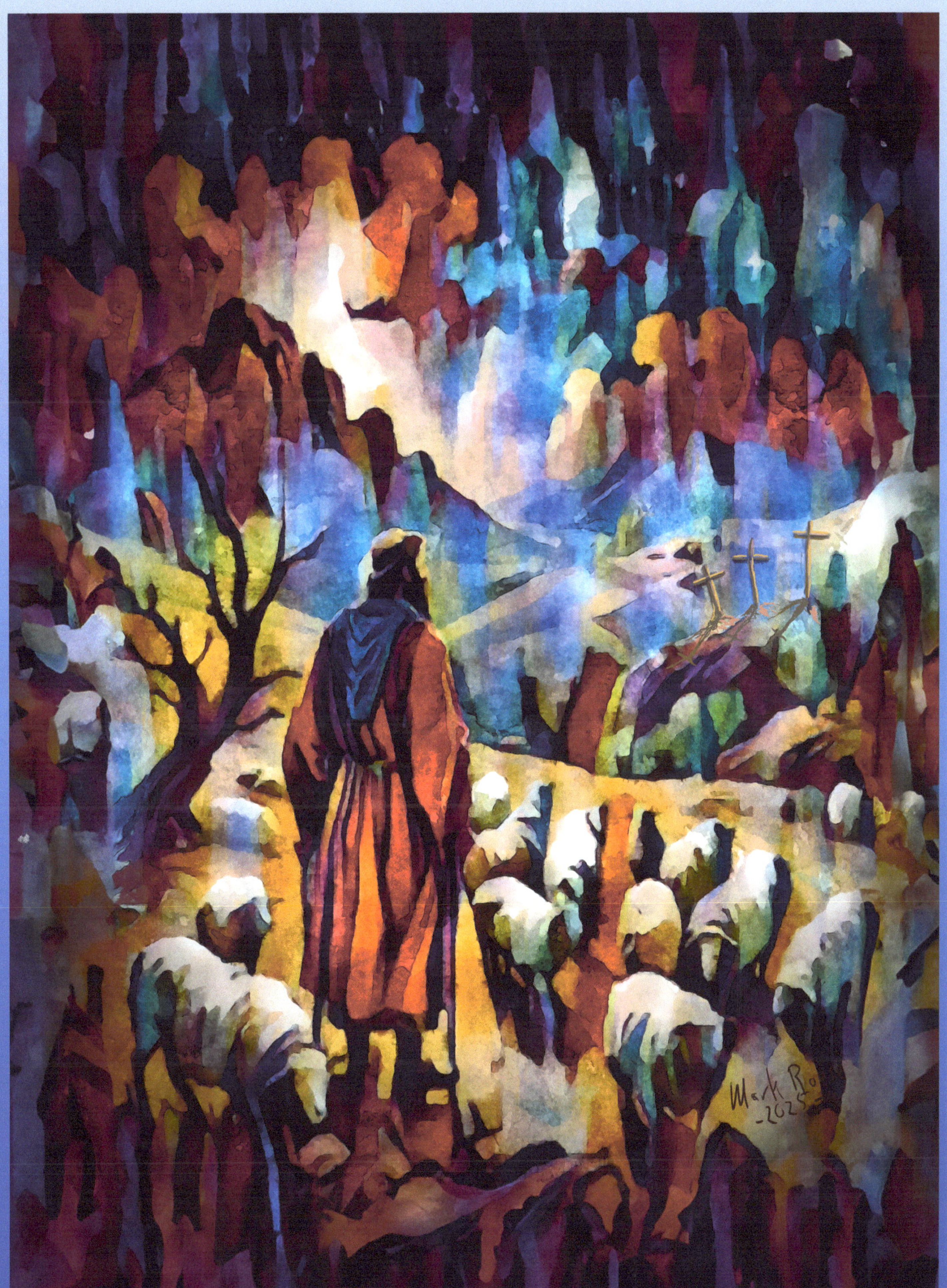

I AM...

...the Bread of Life

Jesus said to them, "I am the bread of life; the one who comes to Me will not be hungry, and the one who believes in Me will never be thirsty. But I said to you that you have indeed seen Me, and yet you do not believe."   **John 6:35-36 NASB**

Bread of Life is a mixed media work that centers on Jesus at the Last Supper, holding up a piece of bread to signify His impending sacrifice. This powerful gesture, with one finger raised and pointing upward, embodies spiritual authority and invites deep reflection on the profound meaning behind His words, "I am the Bread of Life." The artwork draws deeply from rich Christian symbolism, emphasizing bread as not only daily sustenance but also as the body broken and given for the salvation and healing of humanity.

Rendered in vibrant reds, blues, yellows, and greens, the piece creates a luminous, stained-glass effect that breathes life into Jesus' face and flowing robe through bold brushstrokes and dynamic color patches. The composition conveys both intensity and reverence, capturing a moment of spiritual significance with expressive vibrancy. The raised bread features a subtle yet poignant detail—a small stream of blood—reminding viewers of the sacrifice made and the promise of spiritual renewal that flows from it. Through this intimate moment frozen in time, the work encourages a meditation on faith, grace, and the sustaining power of Christ's sacrifice, highlighting how this spiritual nourishment transcends the physical and sustains the soul daily, offering healing and salvation to all who believe.

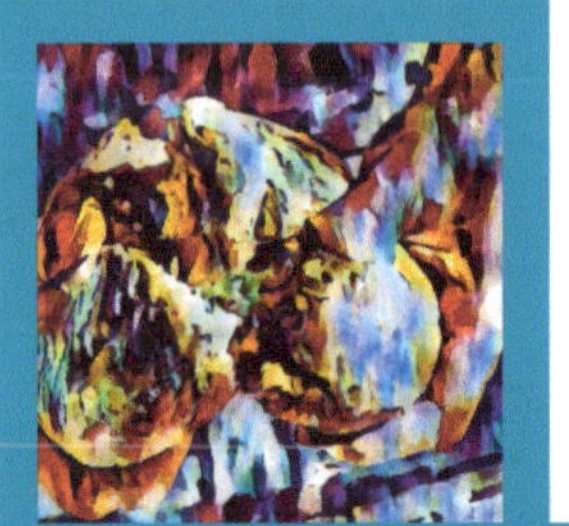

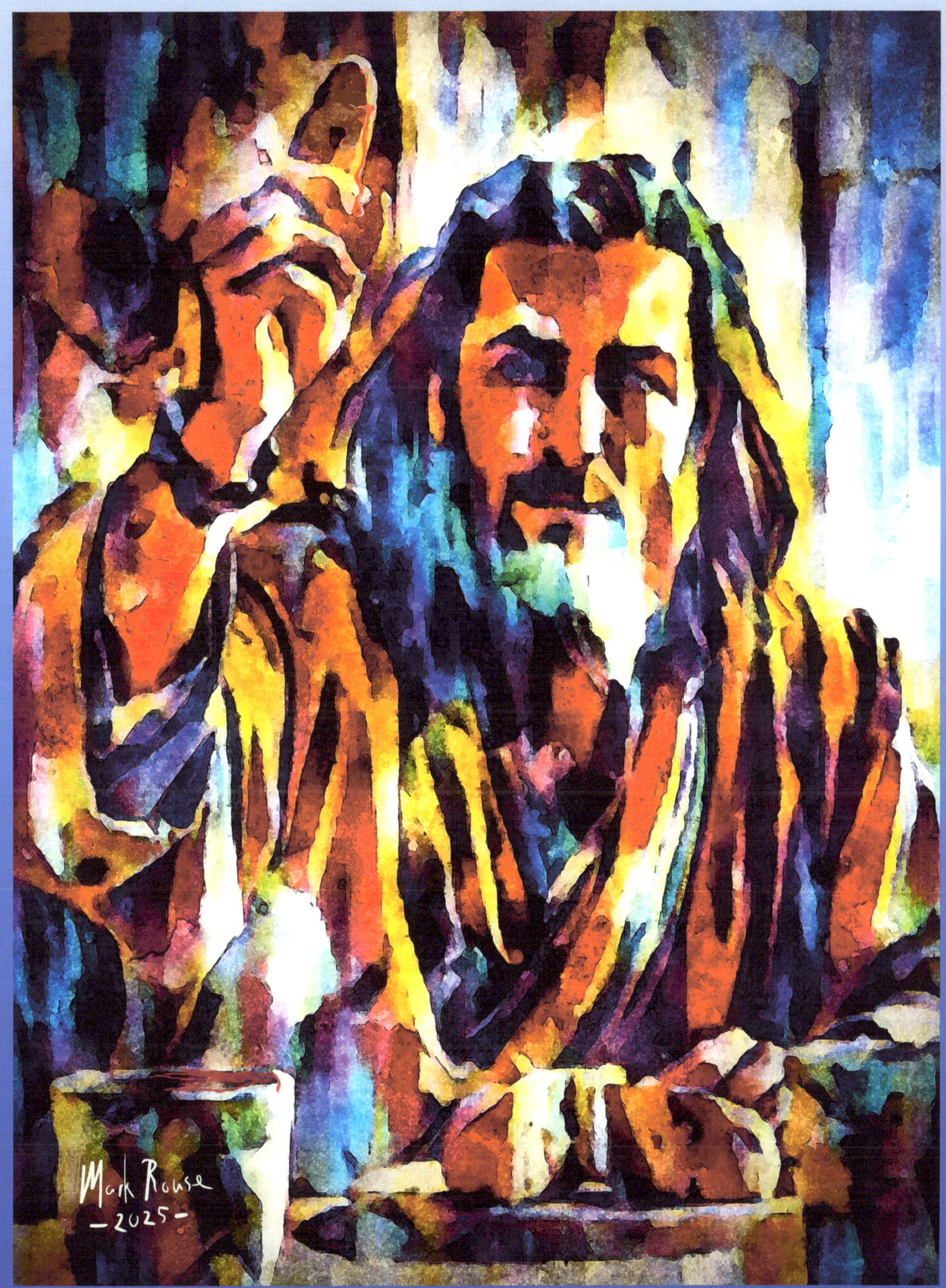
Mark Rouse
-2025-

I AM...

...the Way, the Truth and the Life

Jesus said to him, "I am the way, and the truth, and the life; no one comes to the Father except through Me. If you had known Me, you would have known My Father also; from now on you know Him, and have seen Him."
John 14:6-7 NASB

The Way, the Truth and the Life is a profound spiritual exploration of Christ's sacrifice and the divine promise it embodies. At its heart stands Christ, His hands outstretched and nailed to the cross, a powerful symbol of surrender and love. This vivid portrayal captures the essence of Jesus' declaration, "I AM the Way, the Truth and the Life," inviting viewers into the sacred mystery of redemption and eternal hope.

Christ's form is composed of bold, fragmented shapes in warm hues of red, orange, yellow, and purple, conveying both the intensity of His suffering and the profound depth of His divine presence. The figure's dynamic, urgent depiction speaks to the rawness of the crucifixion—the physical and spiritual anguish endured for the salvation of humanity.

Behind Christ, vertical strokes of blues, greens, and purples create a layered, stained-glass-like backdrop where light and shadow mingle. This rich interplay emphasizes the contrast between pain and promise, death and resurrection, inviting reflection on the transformative power of Christ's obedient sacrifice. The entire composition pulses with spiritual intensity, capturing the decisive moment when Jesus proclaimed, "It is finished," fulfilling the Gospel through His self-giving act.

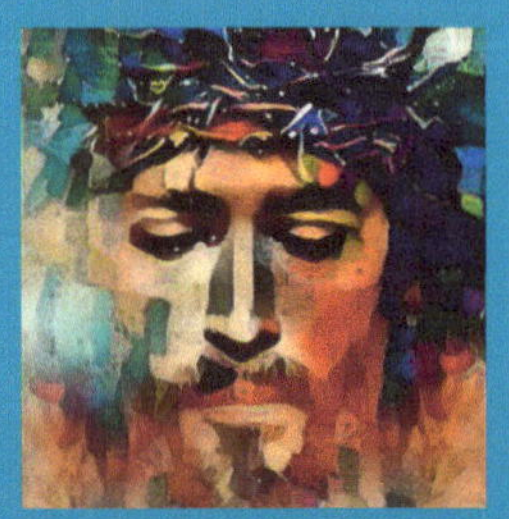

The Way, the Truth and the Life is a vivid meditation on obedience, love, and grace—a work that challenges the viewer to engage deeply with the core of Christian faith, confronting both the agony and the glory of the cross.

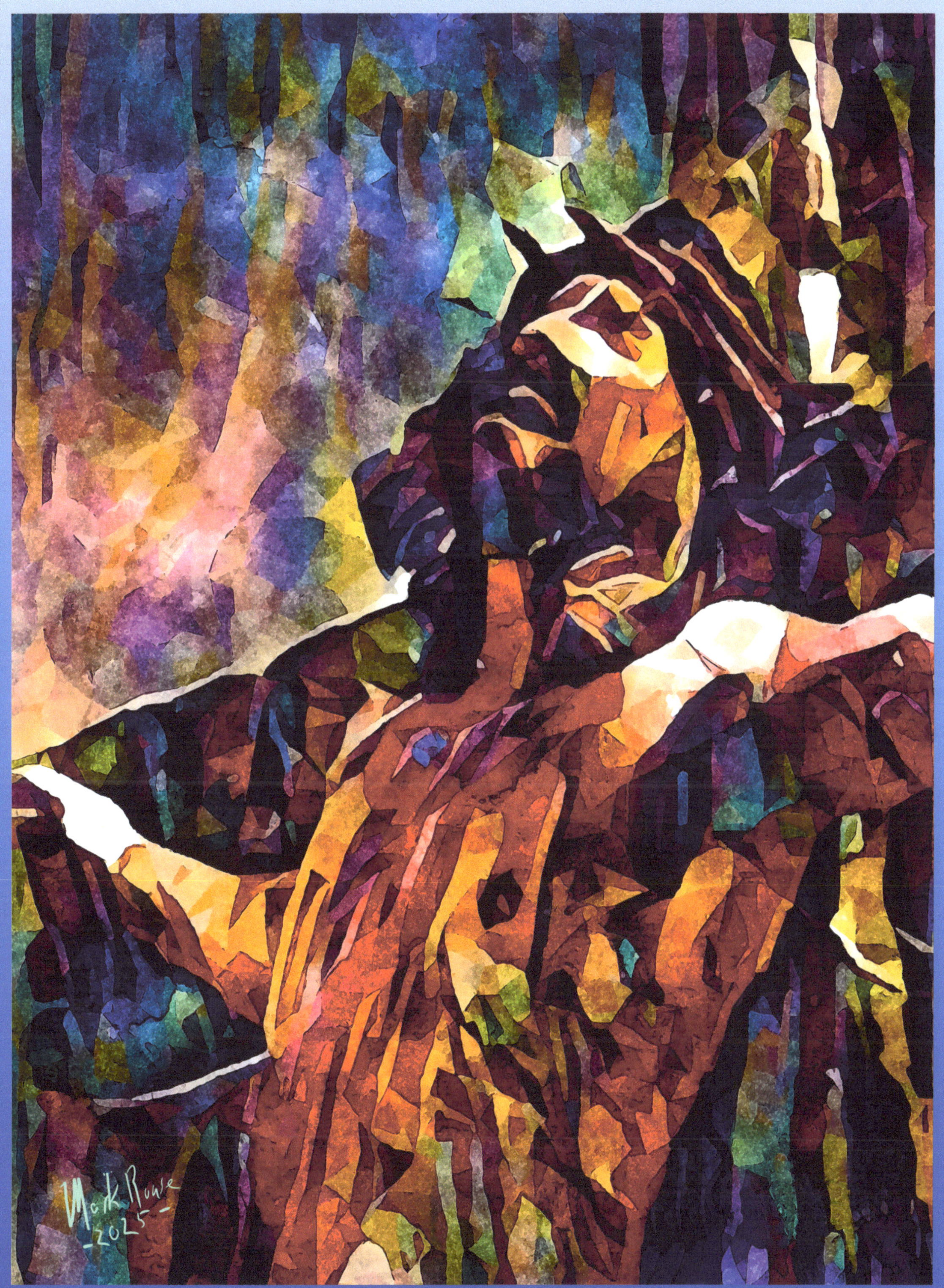
Mark Rowe
2025

I AM...

...the Resurrection and the Life

Jesus said to her, "I am the resurrection and the life; the one who believes in Me will live, even if he dies, and everyone who lives and believes in Me will never die. Do you believe this?" **John 11:25-26 NASB**

The Resurrection and the Life explores the profound spiritual significance of Christ's victory over death and the promise of eternal life. At the heart of the composition is Jesus, portrayed during His Ascension, standing triumphantly atop a mountain. With one arm raised high, He embodies the fulfillment of His declaration as the Resurrection and the Life, a divine figure who transcends time and ushers in a new covenant of grace.

Executed in mixed media, the composition weaves together bold, impressionistic brushstrokes and fragmented shapes that animate the scene with movement and depth. The palette, a vibrant interplay of warm golds, reds, and browns contrasted with cooler blues and purples, evokes a dynamic spiritual landscape where light and shadow coexist. This layering amplifies the sense of cosmic significance, inviting contemplation on the passage from law to grace—the pivotal moment when resurrection redefined covenant and hope.

Within the painting, figures dispersed throughout the composition suggest a communal spiritual journey. Some emerge in the clouds, symbolizing the beginning of eternal life, while others reach upward, seeking salvation and connection to the central presence. The subtle references to the Ascension and the anticipation of return frame the work as both an affirmation of resurrection and a hopeful forward gaze toward fulfillment.

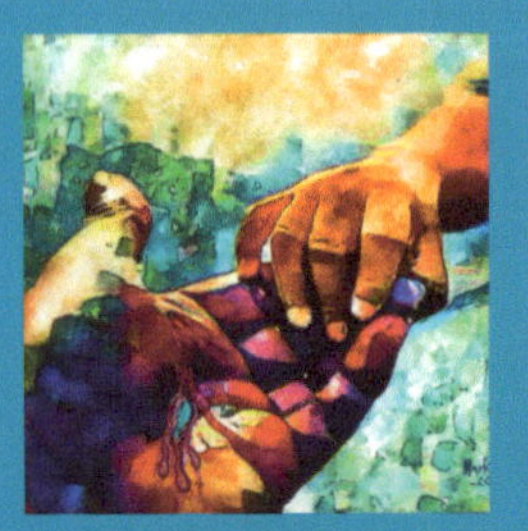

More than an image, this mixed media piece offers a visual sermon on strength, leadership, and divine promise. It calls viewers into reflection on the transformative power inherent in resurrection, underscoring a timeless message of renewal, grace, and the enduring presence of life beyond death.

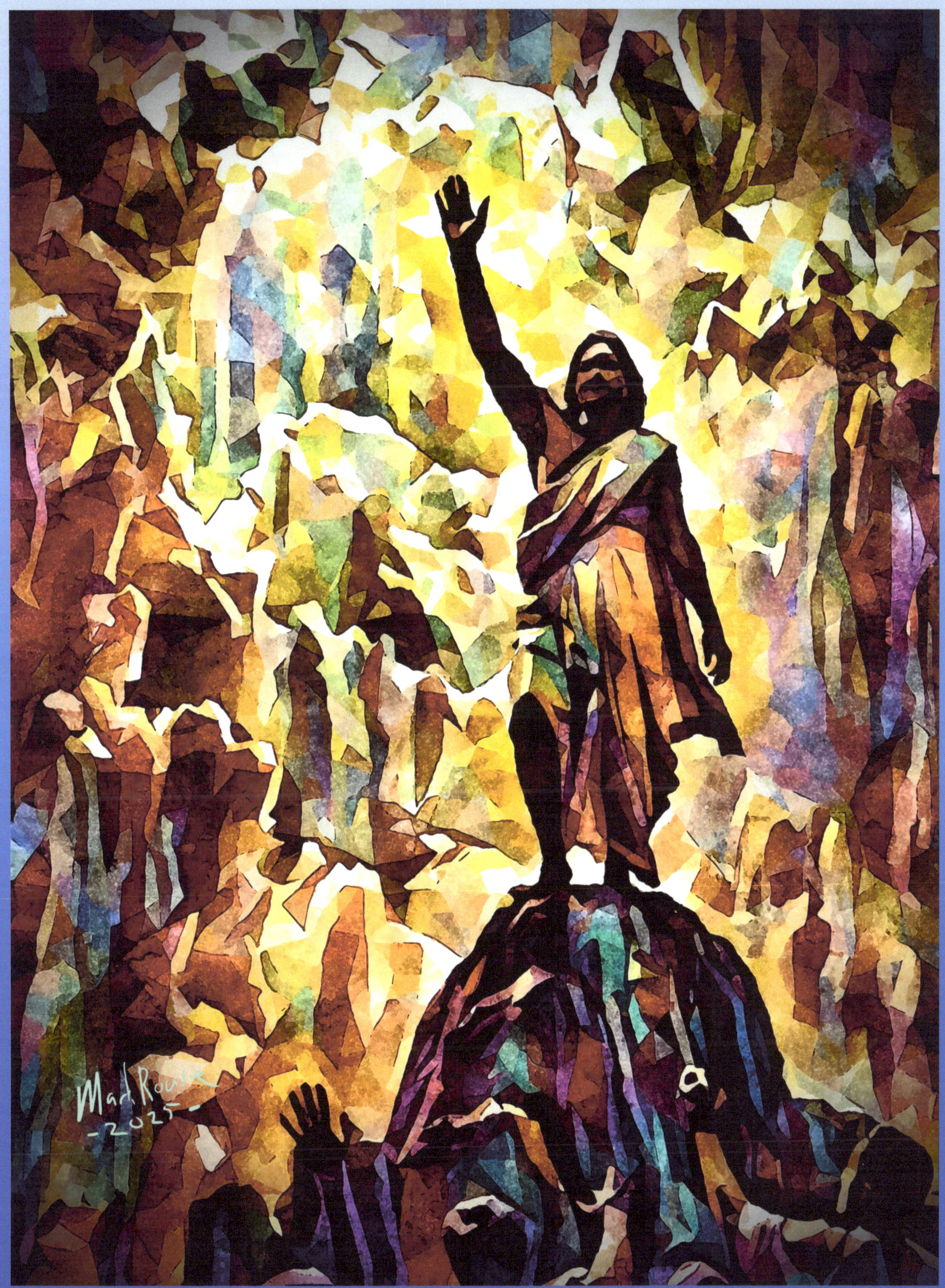

Just Call Me Mark….

After years of studying, teaching and creating art, mostly acrylic paintings, I was diagnosed with diabetic retinopathy.

I was pronounced legally blind!

One of the things that I feared the most was that I would never paint again. I started looking for a way to create, in spite of my diminished vision. This led to my current technique – which involves mixed media and highly tactile, textured surfaces.

Now, my vision is back to normal. With the help of a very good doctor and a couple miracles along the way, my vision was restored.

This painting was done as a gift to the doctor who was key in my treatment and was displayed in an exhibit themed "The Healing Power of Art". The image at the top was what I could see for most of 2015. The next one down was 2016. The third from the top is 2017, when I started painting again. The bottom shows my current vision, illustrating my miraculous recovery.

Both the American Academy of Ophthalmology and Scientific American Magazine have done articles documenting my journey.

Now, I am honored to have been given a platform to help inform people about the dangers of diabetes and the graciousness of a God who loves us.

email—mark@markrouse.com

website - www.markrouseart.com

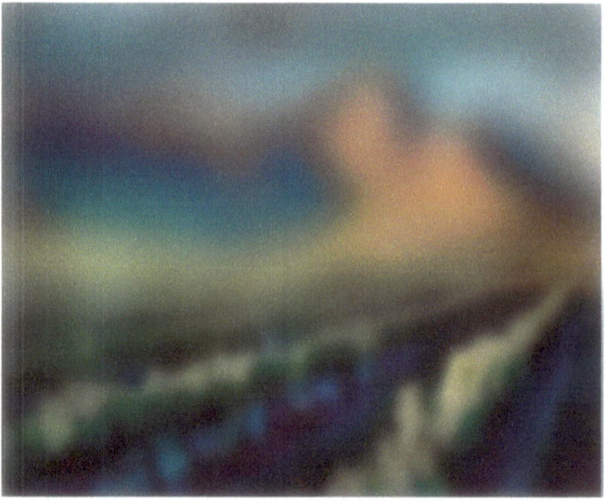
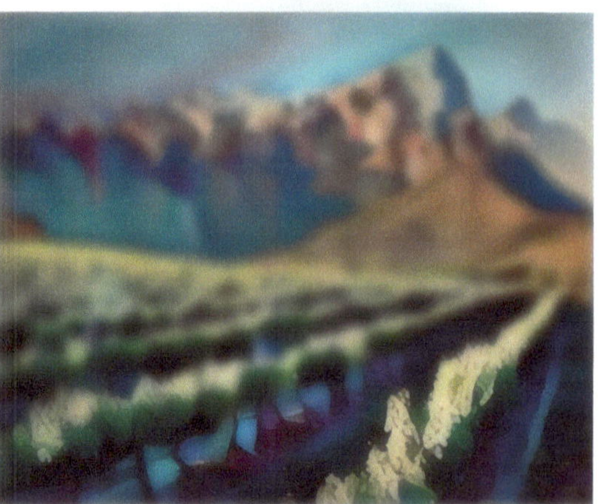
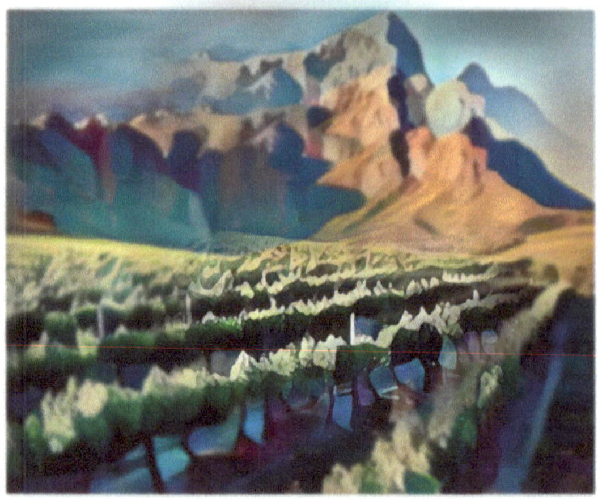
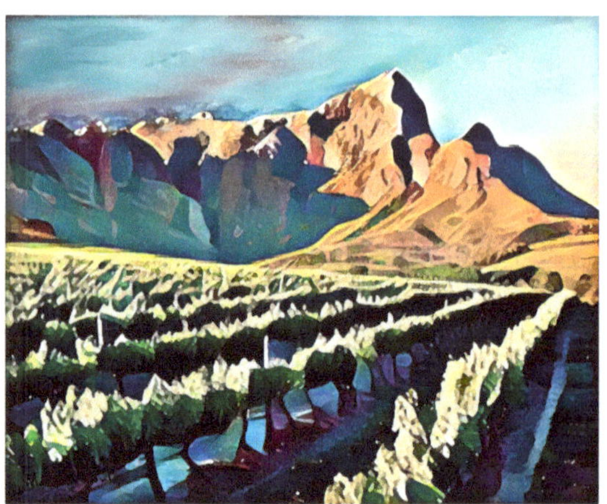

Notes & Thoughts

Poems & Prayers